✔ KU-486-658

# CONTENTS

# EXPLODING MONKEYS AND WONKY DONKEYS

What do you call an
exploding monkey?
A ba-boom.

What's the fittest animal
in the jungle?
A gym-panzee.

What do you call a donkey
with three legs?
A wonky donkey.

What's the fastest gorilla
in the jungle?
King Kong-cord.

**What do you call a flying skunk?**
A smelly-copter.

**What did the frog order
at McDonald's?**
French flies and a diet Croak.

**Why do monkeys have big noses?**
Because they've got big fingers.

**Where do tadpoles go
to change?**
The croakroom.

What's grey and wears
glass slippers?
Cinder-elephant!

What is a toad's favourite ballet?
Swamp lake.

What looks like half a cat?
The other half.

What type of monkey can fly?
A hot air baboon.

What do you call a dog with a cold?

A choo-wawa.

Where do monkeys pick up wild rumours?

On the apevine.

What do whales watch on TV?

Big Blubber.

What did the banana say to the monkey?

Nothing. Bananas can't talk.

Which eel invaded Britain?

William the Conger.

What do monkeys do for laughs?

They tell people jokes.

What animal should you never play cards with?

A cheetah.

How do monkeys get down the stairs?

They slide down the banana-ster.

What happened to the frog that parked on double yellow lines?

He was toad away.

What TV programme does a cat watch every day?

The 6 o'clock Mews.

When are most frogs born?

In a leap year.

What's green with red spots?

A frog with chicken pox.

What goes 'tick-tock-woof'?
A watchdog.

What's green and dangerous?
A frog with a gun.

Which cat discovered
America?
Christopher Colum-puss.

What does a frog say when
it sees something great?
'Toadly awesome!'

Why did the frog go to
the hospital?
He needed a hop-eration.

When is it bad luck to see
a black cat?
When you are a mouse!

Why do dogs wag their tails?
Because no one else will do it
for them.

What did the snake's school
report say?
'His reading is poor but his
writhing is excellent.'

What do you call a mad
sea creature?
A crazy, mixed-up squid.

How do whales communicate?
By sea-mail.

Cow: 'Moo.'
Second cow: 'I was going
to say that!'

What kind of shark does not
eat women?
A man-eating shark.

What do you give a deaf fish?
A herring aid.

What's the safest way to observe shark behaviour?
On TV!

Where would you weigh a whale?
At a whale-weigh station.

What's a shark's favourite game?
Swallow the leader.

What would you find in the middle of a jellyfish?
Its jelly-button.

Who is captain of the Fish Football Squad?

The team's kipper.

What do you call a rabbit's mobile home?

A wheel-burrow.

What do you give a pig with a rash?

Oink-ment.

What's a rabbit's favourite music?
Hip-hop.

What did the rabbit say to the carrot?
It's been nice gnawing you.

How many sheep does it take to make a jumper?
It depends how fast they knit.

What do you call an elephant at the North Pole?
Lost.

What do you get when you cross a pig with a centipede?

Bacon and legs.

Where do cows eat their lunch?

In a calf-eteria.

What do you call a cow with three legs?

Lean beef.

How do you make a baby snake cry?

Take away its rattle.

What do you get if you sit under a cow?

A pat on the head.

What do cows read their calves at bedtime?

Dairy tales.

What happened when the cow jumped over the barbed wire fence?

It was an udder catastrophe.

What do you get when a cow has hiccups?

Milkshake.

How does a lion like his steak?
Medium roar.

How do you know if there is
an elephant under your bed?
Your nose is touching
the ceiling.

What's a lion's favourite
day of the week?
Chews-day.

What would you do if you
found a poisonous snake in
your toilet?
Wait until he's finished!

Where does a grizzly bear go on his birthday?
Anywhere he likes.

What's the difference between a teenager and a leopard?
One's covered in spots and sleeps all day and the other is a leopard.

Why do cows have bells?
Because their horns don't work.

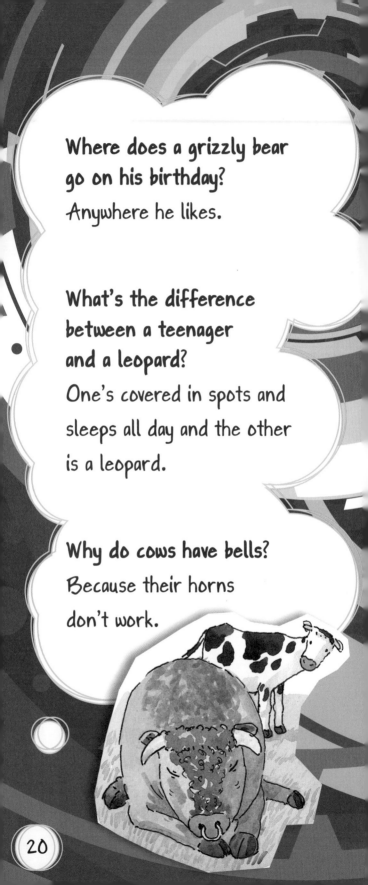

What's an elephant's favourite sport?

Squash.


**Knock, knock.**

Who's there?

**Dozen owl go.**

Dozen owl go who?

**Yes, it does.**


**Which snakes are best at maths?**

Adders.


**Why is it hard to fool a snake?**

Because you can't pull its leg.

What do you call a bear
with a missing ear?
A 'b'!

What did the sick chicken say?
'Oh no, I've got people-pox!'

Why does a flamingo stand
on one leg?
Because if it lifted up the
other one it would fall over.

What do you call
a dead parrot?
A poly-gon.

What do penguins wear when
it's cold?
Ice caps.

Why do hummingbirds hum?
Because they don't know
the words.

What do you get when you run
over a budgie with a lawnmower?
Shredded Tweet.

What did the duck say when he'd
finished shopping?
'Put it on my bill, please!'

What's a parrot's favourite game?
Hide and Speak.

What do you give a sick canary?
Tweetment.

What do you call
a cheerful kangaroo?
A hop-timist.

What's a hedgehog's
favourite food?
Prickled onions.

What happened to the
shy tortoise?
He wouldn't come out
of his shell.

What do you call a pig
rolling in cash?
Filthy rich.

What do call a train
driven by a snail?
A slow-comotive.

Where do gerbils go on holiday?
Hamster-dam.

Why did the pony cough?
Because he was a little horse.

What do you call a camel
with three humps?
Humphrey.

What's the fastest fish
in the lake?
A motor-pike.

How do you save
a drowning mouse?
Give it mouse-to-mouse
resuscitation.

What happened to the lion who
turned into a cannibal?
He swallowed his pride.

What do you call a three-metre
tall mouse?
Enor-mouse.

Why couldn't the two elephants
go swimming together?
Because they only had one pair
of trunks.

What do you get if you cross
a grizzly bear with a wizard?
Hairy Potter.

When do elephants have eight legs?

When there are two of them.

Knock, knock.

Who's there?

Cows.

Cows who?

Cows moo, not who.

What do you give an elephant with a tummy upset?

Lots of room.

What do you get if you cross an elephant with a whale?

A submarine with
a built-in snorkel.

What do you get if you cross a kangaroo with a triceratops?

A tricera-hops.

What would happen if worms took over the planet?

Global worming.

What do you get if you cross a snake with a JCB?

A boa constructor.

What do you get if you cross a dog with a mobile phone?

A golden receiver.

What sound do porcupines make when they kiss?

'Ouch!'

# MUSCLE SPROUTS AND SCREAM CHEESE

What is James Bond's favourite food?

Mince spies.

What are the strongest vegetables in the world?

Muscle sprouts.

'Waiter, will my pizza be long?'

'No, it'll be round, the same as everyone else's!'

What's the best way to see flying saucers?

Trip up the waitress.

Why did the cheese play roulette all night?

Because he was on a roll.

'Waitress, do you serve crabs?'

'Certainly, sir — we serve anyone.'

Why did the baby strawberry cry?

Because his parents were in a jam.

What is a nun's favourite food?

Angel cake.

'Waiter, this soup tastes funny'

'So why aren't you laughing?'

What do monsters have on their toast?

Scream cheese.

What's white and squashy and swings through the jungle?
A meringue-utan.

How does a penguin make pancakes?
With his flippers.

'Waiter, do you have frogs' legs?'
'No, sir, I've always walked like this.'

How do you make fairy cakes?
With elf-raising flour.

Knock, knock.
Who's there?
Orange.
Orange who?
Orange you going to let me in?

Why did the bacon groan?
Because the egg's yolks
were so bad.

Customer: 'What's this?'
Waiter: 'It's a banana surprise.'
Customer: 'I can't see
any bananas.'
Waiter: 'I know, sir, that's
the surprise.'

Mum: 'Eat your spinach, it'll
put colour in your cheeks.'
Max: 'But I don't want
green cheeks!'

What's a Frenchman's
favourite pudding?
Trifle tower.

**Waiter:** 'How did you find your dinner?'
**Customer:** 'With a magnifying glass.'

What happened to the man who stole an apple pie?
He was taken into custard-y.

A man who works in a butcher's shop is 6 feet tall and wears size 11 shoes. What does he weigh?
Meat.

'Waiter, there's a fly in my soup!'
'Don't worry, sir, the spider in your salad will eat it.'

What sits in the corner of the room and wobbles?

A jelly-vision.

Why did the lettuce blush?

He saw the salad dressing.

'Waiter, there's a flea in my soup.'

'Well, tell it to hop it.'

Why did the grape go out with a prune?

Because he couldn't get a date.

What's the difference between British ice cream and American ice cream?

About 5,000 kilometres.

Knock, knock.
Who's there?
Noah.
Noah who?
Noah way to the nearest burger bar?

'Waiter, there's a fly in my coffee.'
'That's all right, sir, he won't drink much.'

Why did the bagel go to the dentist?
Because it needed a filling.

What is a taxi driver's favourite food?
Corn on the cab.

'Waiter, there's a fly swimming in my soup.'
'What do you expect me to do? Call a lifeguard?'

What two things can you never have for breakfast?
Lunch and dinner.

What do you call two banana skins?
A pair of slippers.

'Waiter, there's a small slug in this lettuce.'
'Sorry, sir, I'll just go and get you a bigger one.'

How do you make a sausage roll?
Push it off your plate.

What do you get if you pour boiling water down a rabbit hole?
Hot cross bunnies.

'Waiter, how are your mussels today?'
'A bit sore, sir — I was playing football last night.'

What's a nuclear scientist's favourite food?
Fission chips.

What does a dustbin man have for lunch?
Junk food.

'Waiter, is there spaghetti on the menu?'
'Yes, I'll just get a cloth and wipe it off.'

Tom: 'What've you got in your truck?'
Farmer: 'Horse manure.'
Tom: 'What are you going to do with it?'
Farmer: 'Put it on my strawberries.'
Tom: 'Try cream and sugar — it tastes much better.'

Did you hear about the fight in the chip shop last night?
Two fish got battered.


'Waiter, there's a dead fly in my soup.'
'Looks like he's committed insecticide!'


What did the nut say when it sneezed?
'Ca-shew!'


'Waiter, how often do you change the tablecloths in this restaurant?'
'I don't know, sir, I've only been here six months.'

What happens if you eat yeast
and shoe polish?
You'll rise and shine
every morning.

What do you call a train
full of caramels?
A chew-chew train.

'Waiter, how long will my
sausages be?'
'About ten to twelve
centimetres if you're lucky!'

Why did the doughnut
go to the dentist?
He needed a filling.

If you hold 9 oranges in one hand and 10 lemons in another, what do you have?

Really big hands.

'Waiter, there's a dead fly swimming in my soup.'

'Don't be ridiculous, dead flies can't swim!'

How do you know carrots are good for your eyes?

Because you never see a rabbit wearing glasses.

What do you get when two peas fight?

Black-eyed peas.

'Waiter, what's this insect in my soup?'
'I dunno, I'm a waiter, not a zoologist!'

What vegetable should you never have on a boat?
A leek.

Knock, knock.
Who's there?
Ice cream.
Ice cream who?
Ice cream if you don't let me in!

Mum: 'Why are you shivering?'
Sam: 'Because you're making me chilli!'

'Waiter, there's a button in my soup.'

'Thank you, sir. I've been looking for that everywhere.'

What's a skeleton's favourite barbecue?

Spare ribs.

Why don't polar bears eat penguins?

Because they can't get the wrappers off.

'Waiter, bring me some lamb chops and make them lean.'
'To the left or right, sir?'

Why are cooks cruel?
Because they beat eggs, whip cream and batter fish.

What do golfers eat for lunch?
Club sandwiches.

'Waiter, there's a spider drowning in my soup.'
'I don't think it's deep enough for him to drown, sir.'

Mum: 'Why are you eating so fast?'
Ali: 'I don't want to lose my appetite.'

Why did the man throw his toast out of the window? To watch his butterfly.

Customer: 'What do you call this?'
Waiter: 'It's bean soup, sir.'
Customer: 'I don't care what it's been, what is it know?'

What is small, wobbly and sits in a pram?
A jelly baby

Two crisps were walking down the road when a car stopped. 'Do you want a lift?' asked the driver. 'No thanks,' said one crisp, 'we're Walkers.'

Knock, knock.
Who's there?
Annie.
Annie who?
Annie more biscuits left?
I'm starving!


'Waiter, there's a worm
on my plate.'
'No, sir, that's your sausage.'


What's green and wears an apron?
A cooking apple.


How do you make a banana shake?
Take it to a scary movie.


'Waiter, do you have frog's legs?'
'Yes, sir.'
'Well, hop over here and
take my order.'

Why didn't the hot dog
win an Oscar?
Because he didn't get
any good rolls.

What's a bear's favourite pasta?
Taglia-teddy.

Customer: 'Waiter, this restaurant
must have a very clean kitchen.'
Waiter: 'Why?'
Customer: 'Because everything
tastes like soap.'

Why did the potato on a
motorbike get arrested?
He broke the spud limit.

How did the elf get indigestion?
He kept gobblin' his dinner.

When should you feed giraffe milk to a baby?
When it's a baby giraffe.

'Waiter, send the chef here. I wish to complain about this disgusting meal.'
'I'm afraid you'll have to wait, sir. He's just popped out for his dinner.'

Knock, knock.
Who's there?
Pete.
Pete who?
Pizza delivery man!

**Farmer:** 'I've got a hen that lays square eggs and talks.'
**Ben:** 'That's amazing! What does she say?'
**Farmer:** 'Ouch.'

What do you get if you cross a rabbit with a cake?
A cream bunny.

What do you get if you cross a prawn and a monkey?
A shrimp-anzee.

What do you call a crate of ducks?
A box of quackers.

What do you get if you cross a cow with a cobra?

A milk snake.

Why did the T-rex eat only raw meat?

Because it didn't know how to cook!

What's a penguin's favourite salad?

Iceberg lettuce.

Why did the polar bear eat a clock?

He was just killing time.

Why did the woolly mammoth
eat a stupid man?

Because someone said he was nuts.


What's a fish's favourite game?

Name that tuna.


What's a dog's favourite food?

Anything that's on your plate.


What's the fastest cake
in the world?

Scone!

What do you get if you cross
a Mars bar with an elk?

A chocolate mousse.

Where do tough chickens
come from?

Hard-boiled eggs.

What fish is good for pudding?

A jellyfish.

What's the fastest vegetable?

The runner bean.

# CLASSROOM CRACKERS AND LOOPY LESSONS

**Teacher:** 'If I take four oranges and cut them into quarters, then add 14 grapes, what would I get?'
**Ravi:** 'Fruit salad, Miss.'

**Teacher:** 'What did you write your project on?'
**Oliver:** 'Paper.'

**What should you eat on sports day?**
Runner beans.

What's the largest table in school?

The multiplication table.

Teacher: 'If I gave you three hamsters, and the next day gave you three more, how many would you have?'

Ruby: 'Seven.'

Teacher: 'Seven?'

Ruby: 'Yes, I've got one already.'

What do elves learn in school?

The elf-abet.

Why is it dangerous to do sums in the jungle?

Because if you add four and four, you get ate!

What's a snake's best subject?

Hiss-tory.

**Teacher:** 'If you had £5 and you asked your dad for another £5, how much would you have?'

**Jack:** 'Five pounds.'

**Teacher:** 'You don't know how to add up!'

**Jack:** 'You don't know my dad.'

What's a butterfly's favourite subject?

Mothematics!

**Teacher:** 'Tell me an animal that lives in Lapland.'

**Charlie:** 'A reindeer.'

**Teacher:** 'Good, now tell me another one.'

**Charlie:** 'Another reindeer!'

Why was the cannibal expelled from school?

He kept buttering up the teacher.


How do dinosaurs pass exams?

With extinction.


**Alex:** 'Dad, can you help me find the answer for my maths homework?'

**Dad:** 'Is it still missing? I remember looking for it when I was at school!'


What's a bird's favourite subject?

Owl-gebra!


**Teacher:** 'If there are eight cats in a basket and one jumps out, how many are left?'

**Ed:** 'None. The rest were copycats!'

**Teacher:** 'Where would you find Hadrian's Wall?'
**Tom:** 'Around Hadrian's garden, sir?'

What's a cow's favourite subject?
Moo-sic!

**Teacher:** 'Who built the Ark?'
**Jess:** 'I have Noah idea!'

**Dad:** 'Why aren't you doing very well in history?'
**George:** 'Because the teacher keeps asking about things that happened before I was born!'

What's a pirate's favourite subject?
Arrrr-t!

**Teacher:** 'Why was Oliver Cromwell buried in Westminster Abbey?'
**Joseph:** 'Because he was dead.'

**Teacher:** 'Where was the Magna Carta signed?'
**Lily:** 'At the bottom!'

What's the fastest country in the world?
Rush-a!

**Teacher:** 'Did the Ancient Romans hunt bears?'
**Edward:** 'Not in the winter, if they had any sense.'

**Teacher:** 'What happened at the Boston Tea Party?'
**Grace:** 'I don't know, I wasn't invited.'

What do you call Australian boxer shorts?
Down-underwear!

What is the healthiest lesson?
History, because it's full of dates.

**Teacher:** 'Is eating chicken good for your health?'
**Dan:** 'Not if you're a chicken.'

Where do fish come from?
Fin-land.

**Teacher:** 'Jack, are you sleeping in my class?'
**Jack:** 'Not any more, Miss!'

**Teacher:** 'Why don't you write more neatly?'
**James:** 'Because then you'll be able to see that I can't spell!'

Where do sea mammals come from?
Whales.

What do you call someone that keeps talking when no one is listening?
A teacher.

**Alfred:** 'Mum, please don't make me go to school today. I hate it!'
**Mum:** 'You have to go — after all, you are the headmaster!'

Where do ponies come from?
Horse-tralia.

**Joe to music teacher:** 'What would you like me to play?'
**Teacher:** 'Truant!'

**Why was the teacher cross-eyed?**
She couldn't control her pupils.

**Teacher:** 'Did you take a bath this morning?'
**Luke:** 'No, is there one missing?'

**Where do polar bears come from?**
Chilly.

**Teacher:** 'Why can't you answer any of my questions?
**Emily:** 'Well, if I could there wouldn't be much point in me being here!'

**Where do pigs come from?**
Ham-erica.

**Teacher:** 'If you put your hand in your left pocket and found £1.75 and then put your hand in your right pocket and found £2.50, what would you have?'
**Harry:** 'Somebody else's trousers on!'

**Teacher:** 'This homework is in your mum's handwriting!'
**Ethan:** 'I know, I borrowed her pen.'

Where do pigeons come from?
Coo-lumbia.

Jack: 'My teacher's an angel.'
Alfie: 'You're lucky. Mine's
still alive!'

Teacher: 'What is a duchess?'
Joe: 'I dunno — is it different
to an English "S"?'

Where do wasps come from?
Sting-apore.

Teacher: 'Where is the
English Channel?'
Pupil: 'I don't know, I haven't
got digital TV!'

Where do girls come from?
Skirt-land.

**Arnie:** 'My teacher was bitten by a dog yesterday.'
**Ben:** 'How is she?'
**Arnie:** 'She's fine, but the dog died.'

**Teacher:** 'I hope I didn't see you looking at Jack's answers!'
**Harry:** 'I hope you didn't, too.'

**Teacher:** 'Lewis, did you miss school yesterday?'
**Lewis:** 'No, I didn't miss it at all!'

Where do you go to learn how to make ice cream?
Sundae school!

**Teacher:** 'You aren't paying attention to me. Are you having trouble hearing?'
**Sophie:** 'No, Miss — I'm having trouble listening.'

**Teacher:** 'You've got your shoes on the wrong feet.'
**Adam:** 'These are the only feet I've got, sir.'

**What do goblins drink with their school lunch?**
Lemon 'n' slime.

**Teacher:** 'Which word is always spelt wrong?'
**Lily:** 'Wrong!'

What do you call the biggest bully in the playground?
Lord of the Swings.

**Teacher:** 'Can you name two days of the week beginning with the letter "T"?'
**Jacob:** 'Er, today and tomorrow?'

**Teacher:** 'What time did you wake up this morning, Joe?'
**Joe:** 'About 10 minutes after I got to school, sir!'

Why was Cinderella dropped from the school football team?

Because she ran away from the ball.

**Teacher:** 'Dylan, stop humming while you're working!'
**Dylan:** 'I'm not working, Miss, just humming!'

**Teacher:** 'What do you call a tree that loses its leaves?'
**Hannah:** 'Careless?'

**Why did the thermometer go to college?**
Because he wanted to get a degree.

**Teacher:** 'Name a liquid that will never freeze.'
**Samuel:** 'Hot water.'

**Teacher:** What do you find at the end of a rainbow?
**Callum:** 'The letter "w".'

**Teacher:** 'You should have been here at 9 o'clock.'
**Tom:** 'Why, did something exciting happen?'

**Why did the boy eat his homework?**
Because the teacher told him it was a piece of cake.

**Teacher:** 'You weren't at school yesterday, Alex. I heard you were at the cinema.'
**Alex:** 'That's not true — I've got the tickets from the football match to prove it!'

**Teacher:** 'Why are you always late for school?'
**Matthew:** 'Because you always ring the bell before I get here!'

**Why did the kid walk backwards to school?**
It was back-to-school day.

**Teacher:** 'This essay about your pet parrot is exactly the same as the one your sister handed in!'
**Amelia:** 'Yes, Miss, it's the same parrot.'

**Teacher:** 'What was the Romans' most remarkable achievement?'
**Ellie:** 'Learning Latin!'

**What did the dinosaur have for lunch at school?**
The headteacher.

**Dad:** 'What did you learn in school today?'
**Daniel:** 'I learned that those sums you did for me were wrong.'

**Charlie:** 'I've been banned from cookery lessons because I burned something.'
**Mum:** 'What did you burn?'
**Charlie:** 'I burned the school down.'


**Dad:** 'What did you learn today?'
**Daniel:** 'I learned that those sums you did for me were wrong.'


**What did the bookworm say to the librarian?**

'Can I burrow this book, please?'


**Harvey:** 'How many teachers work at this school?'
**Henry:** 'About half of them!'

What insect is good at maths?
An account-ant.

Teacher: 'If an apple a day keeps the doctor away, what does an onion do?'
Freddy: 'Keeps everyone away!'

Ryan: 'How did you manage to get that black eye?'
Jamie: 'You see that tree in the playground?'
Ryan: 'Yes.'
Jamie: 'Well, I didn't.'

Teacher: 'I hear you've been telling everyone that I'm boring.'
Harrison: 'Sorry, I didn't know it was meant to be a secret.'

**Teacher:** 'Why are a lot of famous artists Dutch?'
**Tom:** 'Because they were born in Holland!'

**Teacher:** 'That story's excellently written for someone your age!'
**Ella:** 'How about for someone my mum's age?'

Who would you find on a haunted beach during the school holidays?
Sand-witches.

How did the Vikings send secret messages?
By Norse code.

Dad: 'How were the exam questions?'
Molly: 'Fine.'
Dad: 'Why are you crying then?'
Molly: 'The questions were fine. The answers were the problem.'

Josh: 'How old is Professor Pratt?'
Sam: 'Really old. He told me he used to teach Shakespeare!'

What do you call a Victorian ant?
An antique.

Owen (on phone): 'Owen has a bad cold and won't be able to come to school today.'
School secretary: 'Who is this?'
Owen: 'This is my dad speaking.'

Teacher: 'Are you good at arithmetic?'
Nathan: 'Well, yes and no.'
Teacher: 'What do you mean, yes and no?'
Nathan: 'Yes, I'm no good at arithmetic.'

Why did the chicken cross the playground?
To get to the other slide.

**Mum:** 'What did you learn in school today?'
**Will:** 'How to write.'
**Mum:** 'What did you write?'
**Will:** 'I don't know, they haven't taught us how to read yet!'

**Abigail:** 'My teacher gave me a detention for something I didn't do!'
**Mum:** 'That's terrible. What didn't you do?'
**Abigail:** 'My homework.'

**Where do ghosts do their homework?**
Exorcise books.

Jake: 'Someone threw a stink bomb into the boys' toilets today.'
Mum: 'How did it smell?'
Jake: 'Much better!'

Holly: 'Why are you going to night school?'
Heidi: 'To learn how to read in the dark!'

What did the alien say to the school librarian?
'Take me to your reader.'

Why was the maths book unhappy?
Because it had loads of problems.

# BIZARRE BOGEYS AND MAD MONSTERS

What's the difference between bogeys and cabbage? Kids don't eat cabbage.

What monster plays the most April Fool's jokes? Prankenstein.

Why did the vampire become an artist? Because he was so good at drawing blood.

What did the nose say
to the boy?
'Why are you always picking
on me?'

What would you call
a friendly monster?
A failure.

What did the policeman say
to his belly button?
'You're under a vest.'

What did the tissue say to
the nose?
'Don't get snotty with me!'

How did the kid catch Egyptian flu?

He caught it from his mummy.

What is Dracula's favourite fruit?

Neck-tarines.

What do you call a smelly fairy?

Stinkerbell.

What's a ghost's favourite ice-cream flavour?

Shock-olate chip.

What happens when Prince William burps?

He gets a royal pardon.

Why didn't the skeleton go bungee-jumping?
He didn't have the guts.

Why was the nose so tired?
Because it had been running all day.

Where did the broken action man go to get fixed?
To the plastic surgeon.

Why do witches wear name tags?
So they know which witch is which.

What monster sits on the end of your finger?
The Bogeyman.

**Why did the seaweed blush?**
Because it saw the ship's bottom.

**What do cannibals eat at picnics?**
Hard-boiled legs.

**How many ears does Captain Kirk have?**
Three. A left ear, a right ear, and a Final Frontier.

**Why did the bogey cross the road?**
Because he was tired of getting picked on.

**What has four wheels and goes, 'Hic! Hic! Hic!'?**
A hiccup truck.

What colour is a hiccup?
Burple.

What has a bottom at the top?
Your legs.

What's brown, hairy and full
of snot?
A coconut with a cold.

What did one eye say
to the other?
'Between you and me,
something smells!'

What do you get if King Kong sits
on your piano?
A flat note.

**Where do ghost trains stop?**
At devil crossings.

**Why did the boy blush when he opened the fridge?**
He saw the salad dressing.

**Dentist:** 'Have your teeth ever been checked?'
**Tom:** 'No, they've always been white.'

**How do monsters communicate?**
By terror-phone.

**Where do zombies have parties?**
In a rave-yard.

**What has four wheels and flies?**

A rubbish truck.

**What do ghosts do at Christmas?**

They go to a phantomime.

**What do young ghosts write their homework in?**

Exorcise books.

**What do you get if you cross a pudding and a cow pat?**

A smelly jelly.

**Why did the boy carry a clock and a budgie at Halloween?**
So that he could go tick or tweeting.

**What's Dracula's favourite film?**
The Vampire Strikes Back.

**What do vampires read their children at night?**
Bite-time stories.

**Why did the lamp-post blush?**
It saw the traffic light changing.

**What do you call a ghost's mum and dad?**
Transparents.

What happened to the magician who did a show for cannibals?

He went down really well.

What did the ghost say to the vampire?

'Do you believe in people?'

What's Dracula's favourite TV show?

Fiends.

What's Dracula's favourite page in the newspaper?

The horror-scope.

Why do witches use brooms to fly on?

Because vacuum cleaners are too heavy.

What do you get if you cross a skeleton with a cowboy?

The Bone Ranger.

Jack: 'There's a monster at the door with a really ugly face.'

Dad: 'Tell him you've already got one.'

What happened at the cannibal's wedding?

They toasted the bride and groom.

What position did the ghost play in the football team?

Ghoul-keeper.

What was the tall ghost's best position in netball?

Ghoul defence.

What's a skeleton's favourite type of joke?

A rib-tickler.

What would you get if you crossed Halloween with April 1st?

April Ghouls' Day.

What is a vampire's favourite type of boat?

Blood vessels.

How do you know if you've been made upside-down?

Your nose runs and your feet smell.

Why does everyone hate Dracula?

Because he is a pain in the neck.

Who did Frankenstein take to the Halloween party?

His ghoul friend.

What do you get if you cross a cocker spaniel, a poodle and a ghost?

A cocker-poodle-boo.

What is Dracula's favourite ice cream?

Vein-illa.

What do short-sighted ghosts wear?

Spook-tacles.

How does a monster count
to thirteen?
On his fingers.

What do you get when you cross
a snowman with a vampire?
Frostbite.

What's a sea monster's
favourite meal?
Fish and ships.

What do you get if you cross
Godzilla with a dog?

A nervous postman.


What do vampires eat
for breakfast?

Dreaded Wheat.


What do you call a skeleton that
won't get out of bed?

Lazy Bones.


What's a ghost's
favourite dessert?

I scream.


What do you call an
angry monster?

SIR.

What should you do if you find a monster in your bed?

Find somewhere else to sleep.

Why did the witch buy a new computer?

Because it had a spell checker.

Why are mummies the most selfish monsters?

Because they are all wrapped up in themselves.

What happened when the wizard met the witch?

It was love at first fright.

**What does Harry Potter do when he stays in a hotel?**

He calls broom service.

**What do you call a nervous witch?**

A twitch.

**What has webbed feet and fangs?**

Count Quackula.

**What do you get if you cross a bird with a wizard?**

A flying sorcerer.

**What does Dracula do at 11 o'clock every morning?**

Takes a coffin break.

**Boy cannibal:** 'I hate my baby sister.'
**Mum cannibal:** 'Well leave her to one side and just eat your chips.'

**Do zombies eat popcorn with their fingers?**
No, they eat the fingers separately.

**Why couldn't Dracula's wife get to sleep?**
Because of his coffin.

**Boy cannibal:** 'Mum, can I bring my friend over for tea?'
**Mum cannibal:** 'Of course, dear. Put him in the fridge and we'll have him later.'

What is as sharp as a vampire's fang?
His other fang.

Where do vampires keep their savings?
In the blood bank.

What's a ghost's favourite airline?
British Scareways.

What do ants use to smell nice?
Deodor-ant.

What do you call a ghost
who haunts the town hall?
A night mayor.

Where do monsters live?
In a monstro-city.

Why couldn't the skunk use
her phone?
It was out of odour.

**What is round, white and smells really bad?**

A ping-pong ball.

**What do you call a mummy who eats biscuits in bed?**

A crumby mummy.

**What do ghosts eat with roast beef?**

Grave-y.

**Where do ghosts go on holiday?**

The Isle of Fright.

Where does a bee sit?
On his bee-hind.

What do you get if you cross
a worm and a young goat?
A dirty kid.

What do you get if you cross a
Scottish legend with a bad egg?
The Long Ness Pongster.

What do you call a monster
who eats your biscuits?
The Cookie Monster.

What kind of music do mummies listen to?

Wrap.

Why do witches think they're funny?

Every time they look in the mirror, it cracks up.

What do you get if you cross a rabbit with a wolf?

A harewolf.

What's the smelliest city in the United States?

Phew York.

# FRYING SAUCERS AND RIDICULOUS RANDOMS

What do you get if you cross a UFO with a rasher of bacon?

A frying saucer.

Why are Martians good at gardening?

Because they have green fingers.

What happened to the astronaut who reached the moon in nine minutes?

He got into the Guinness Book of Out-of-This-World Records.

Why did Chewbacca go to the doctor?

He had Star Warts.

What does Doctor Who eat with his pasta?
Dalek bread.

What kind of car does Luke Skywalker drive?
A Toy-yoda.

What are aliens' favourite sweets?
Martian-mallows!

Why are astronauts always successful?
Because they go up in the world.

What do you call a flea that lives on the moon?
A lunar-tick.

How does a Martian keep his trousers up?

With an asteroid belt.

What's an alien's favourite cartoon?

Lunar-tunes!

Why did the astronaut get a new job?

Because he got fired.

Where does Dr Who buy his cheese?

At a dalek-atessen.

What do astronauts wear to keep warm?

Apollo neck jumpers.

**What happened to the first restaurant on the moon?**
The food was good, but the place lacked atmosphere.

**What's an astronaut's favourite game?**
Moon-opoly.

**What did the Martian chef find in his cupboard?**
An unidentified frying object.

**Where do astronauts keep their sandwiches?**
In a launch box.

What did the alien say to the gardener?

'Take me to your weeder.'

What did the alien say to the chef?

'Take me to your larder.'

What do you call a crazy space traveller?

An astro-nut!

What did one comet say the other?
'Pleased to meteor!'

What do you say to a dead robot?
'Rust in peace.'

Why do cats hate flying saucers?
Because they can't reach the milk.

What's a scientist's favourite film?
Fission Impossible.

Where did the astronaut leave the spaceship?
At a parking meteor.

How do you stop an astronaut's baby from crying?

Rocket.

Where do Martians go for a night out?

To the Mars Bar.

What kind of star wears sunglasses?

A movie star!

What was the first coffee bar in outer space?

Star-bucks!

Can you spell eighty in two letters?

A.T.

What do you get if you cross
a Martian with a golf score?

A little green bogey.

Why is Sunday stronger
than Monday?

Because Monday is a weak day.

Why did Granny put wheels on her
rocking chair?

She liked to rock and roll.

Who was the first underwater spy?

James Pond.

Where do you find giant snails?

On the end of a giant's fingers.

What did dinosaurs have that no others animals ever had?
Baby dinosaurs.

Why didn't the dinosaur cross the road?
There weren't any roads in those days.

What do you call a terrified dinosaur?
Nervous Rex.

What do dinosaurs use to cut down trees?
Dinosaws.

**Toby:** 'How would you feel if you saw a dinosaur in your garden?'
**Tyler:** 'Very old!'

What do you call a dinosaur with blisters?
My-feet-are-sore-us.

What would you call a dinosaur if you saw one today?
Dead!

What do you get if you cross a dinosaur with Eminem?
A rap-tor!

What do you call a dinosaur
that complains all the time?
A whine-osaur.

What do you call a dinosaur
that never gives up?
A try, try, try-ceratops.

What do you get if you cross
a skunk with a bear?
Winnie the Pooh.

What lies on its back with one
hundred feet in the air?
A dead centipede.

What do you get when you
cross a fish with an elephant?
Swimming trunks.

What do you get when you
cross a parrot with
a centipede?
A walkie-talkie.

What do you get if you cross
an elephant with a kangaroo?
Big holes all over Australia.

What do you get if you cross a
cat with a surgeon?
A doctor-puss.

**What do you get if you cross a duck with a box of matches?**

A fire-quacker.

**What did the woodworm say to the chair?**

'It's been nice gnawing you.'

**Where did the stupid woodworm live?**

In a brick.

**What do you get if you cross a dog and a frog?**

A croaker spaniel.

**What do you do when two snails have a fight?**

Leave them to slug it out.

What has antlers and sucks blood?

A moose-quito!

How do snails get their shells so shiny?

They use snail varnish.

Which insect makes films?

Steven Spielbug.

What is a bee with a low buzz?

A mumble bee.

What do you call a bee that is always complaining?

A grumble bee.

Why was the baby ant
so confused?
Because all its uncles were ants.

How do you start a flea race?
One, two, flea, go!

Why couldn't the butterfly go
to the party?
It was a moth ball.

Why did the bees go on strike?
For more honey and
shorter flowers.

What's a snowman's
favourite song?
Freeze a Jolly Good Fellow.

What do you call a man who
was born in France, lived in
Spain and died in England?
Dead.

Tourist: 'Can you tell me the
way to Bath?'
Max: 'Plenty of soap and
water!'

Charlotte: 'I just flew in from
New York.'
Ella: 'Really? Your arms must
be killing you!'

What do you get if you cross a river and a stream?

Wet!

Why was the sand wet?

Because the sea weed.

What do you call a snowman in the Sahara desert?

A puddle.

**Tourist:** 'How do I get to Wembley Stadium?'

**Police officer:** 'Keep up the training, sir.'

**Lily:** 'Mum, why do I have to go to bed?'
**Mum:** 'Because the bed won't come to you.'

**Lucas:** 'Gran, why do you keep going to look at the letterbox?'
**Gran:** 'Because my computer keeps telling me I've got mail.'

**Matt:** 'Have you ever hunted bears?'
**Grandad:** 'No, but I've been fishing in shorts!'

**Mum:** 'Why are you carrying that umbrella?'
**Ellie:** 'Because it can't walk.'

**Uncle Dave:** 'You're very quiet, Joe.'
**Joe:** 'Well, Mum paid me to not say anything about your massive nose.'

**Mum:** 'Harry, you've been in a fight — you've lost your front teeth!'
**Harry:** 'No I haven't, Mum. They're in my pocket.'

**Mum:** 'Why did you put a mouse in Auntie's bed?'
**George:** 'Because I couldn't find a spider.'

**Dad:** 'What's on the TV?'
**Sam:** 'A bowl of fruit and a vase.'

**Nathan:** 'Gran, why have you got custard in one ear and jelly in the other?'
**Gran:** 'Speak up, dear. I'm a trifle deaf.'

**Dad:** 'Where's your school report?'
**Ben:** 'I haven't got it.'
**Dad:** 'Why not?'
**Ben:** 'My mate borrowed it. He wanted to scare his parents.'

**Old lady:** 'Where were you born?'
**Jamie:** 'London.'
**Old lady:** 'Which part?'
**Jamie:** 'All of me.'


**Alex:** 'I wouldn't want to be in your shoes.'
**Dad:** 'Why not?'
**Alex:** 'They're too big for me.'


**When do mice follow cats?**
In a dictionary.


**Why did the chicken cross the web?**
To get to the other site.

What starts with 'e', ends with 'e' and only has one letter?

An envelope.

What crisps can fly?

Plain crisps.

When do computers go to sleep?

When it's internight.

Why did the tap dancer leave his job?

He kept falling in the sink.

How can you make seven even?
Take away the letter 's'.

What do you call a funny
horse racer?
A jokey.

What's an elf's favourite kind
of birthday cake?
Shortcake.

How do you take a lion's
temperature?
Very carefully.

Where do snowmen put their websites?

On the winternet.

What do you get if you cross a computer with a ballet?

The Netcracker.

How can you double your money?

Look at it in a mirror.

What do you do if you split your sides laughing?

Run until you get a stitch.